*Quick*GUIDES
everything you need to know...fast

Bequests and Legacies

by Margaret Burke

reviewed by Kathryn Aldridge

WIREMILL
PUBLISHING LTD

Across the world the organizations and institutions that fundraise to finance their work are referred to in many different ways. They are charities, non-profits or not-for-profit organizations, non-governmental organizations (NGOs), voluntary organizations, academic institutions, agencies, etc. For ease of reading, we have used the term Nonprofit Organization, Organization or NPO as an umbrella term throughout the *Quick*Guide series. We have also used the spellings and punctuation used by the author.

Published by
Wiremill Publishing Ltd.
Edenbridge, Kent TN8 5PS, UK
info@wiremillpublishing.com
www.wiremillpublishing.com
www.quickguidesonline.com

British Library Cataloguing in Publication Data
A catalogue record for this book is available from the British Library.

ISBN Number 1-905053-09-6

Printed by Rhythm Consolidated Berhad, Malaysia
Cover Design by Jennie de Lima and Edward Way
Design by Colin Woodman Design

CONTENTS

BEQUESTS AND LEGACIES

INTRODUCTION

A bequest, also known as a legacy in some countries, is a gift in a Will or other instrument that takes effect at death. (The word "bequest" will be used in this Guide.)

Bequests are gifts of faith, in an organisation's future. They are made by forward-looking individuals who believe in the nonprofit organisation (NPO) and who want to make a difference in future years. The bequest is the most popular form of planned giving and also one of the most cost-effective forms of fundraising. It allows individuals to make gifts that are much larger than they could give in their lifetimes.

Bequests have long been the cornerstone of donations for many organisations and they often count for a significant portion of an NPO's endowment or recurrent income. Increasingly NPOs promote and manage bequest fundraising proactively rather than view these donations as an unexpected bonus.

This Guide will discuss planning and executing a bequest fundraising programme together with helpful tips to maximize income from this source.

PROCESS OF BEQUEST FUNDRAISING

Instituting and managing a programme of bequest fundraising involves the following process:

- Understanding why people support organisations with bequests and who might be most likely to do so.

- Deciding that a bequest fundraising programme would be valuable and ensuring that appropriate staff are engaged or trained to manage such a programme.

- Raising the profile of the organisation.

- Promoting and marketing the bequest opportunity.

- Researching prospects and determining which ones would be appropriate to solicit for bequests.

- Developing detailed knowledge about forms of bequest giving and the relevant legal and tax issues.

- Producing accessible and user-friendly information for potential bequest donors and influencers.

- Face-to-face meetings to discuss leaving a bequest.

- Maintaining good relationships with donors and influencers.

- Managing information – recording relevant details about prospects and confirmed bequest donors.

- Identifying and networking with key influencers.

- Evaluating the programme's performance.

These areas will all be covered in the following pages.

Reviewer's Comment
Also consider writing an ethics policy as part of your programme before launching your bequest programme so that the NPO board, CEO and staff are in agreement on what is expected in terms of professional conduct and appropriateness.

The specific circumstances that may motivate individuals to make a major gift via their Wills are usually unique to the individuals, but there are a number of common elements that play a part in the process. These are:

- Awareness
- Involvement
- Caring
- Sense of commitment
- Expression of commitment

There are three major factors that influence bequest decisions:

- Personal financial or giving capacity
- Relationship with the NPO
- Relationship with the person seeking the bequest

In addition, fundraisers should be aware of powerful human needs that are often important considerations in the decision to give a major gift:

- The need to memorialise or honour oneself or loved ones.
- The need to perpetuate values or opinions.
- The need to belong.
- The need for recognition or status.
- The need to fulfil perception of duty.

The decision to support a particular NPO will depend on organisational factors (for example, the donor's perception of the organisation's efficiency, effectiveness, reputation, and the quality and relevance of its communications).

Donors must know above all that:

- You are a reputable organisation worthy of their support.
- You have the financial expertise and capacity to manage bequests.
- A bequest to your organisation will make a difference.

The stimulus to give is likely to come from the NPO, a professional advisor, a friend or relative. The role of these external "influencers" is discussed later in this Guide.

PROS AND CONS OF BEQUEST FUNDRAISING

Bequests form a significant proportion of income for many NPOs, and marketing the opportunity proactively can increase this income. Most donors feel that asking for such a gift is appropriate, provided it is done sensitively. However, some NPOs have reservations about bequest fundraising that need to be addressed before a bequest fundraising programme can be instituted.

Bequests make sense to donors because:

■ They are revocable by donors if personal circumstances change or a donor changes his or her mind.

■ They allow donors to support something which they value without an uncomfortable financial burden during their lifetimes.

■ They may reduce estate, inheritance or other taxes for surviving family members.

■ They can provide organisations with sizeable gifts for which the donor receives recognition during his or her lifetime.

■ They can provide a memorial to a donor in perpetuity.

The concept of bequest fundraising can be difficult for an NPO because:

■ CEOs and volunteers see the results of bequest fundraising as too distant when an organisation needs funds now.

■ People are concerned about the implicit connection between death and fundraising and don't like broaching the subject.

■ Approaches might be made to elderly people who can be vulnerable.

■ Fundraisers fear that family members will be offended if the organisation asks for a bequest, or they fear that family members will contest a bequest, involving the organisation in court costs and negative publicity.

Reviewer's Comment
Another problem with bequest fundraising is the inability of NPOs to accurately budget for bequest income.

These concerns are valid but can be managed and overcome.

Promoting the Organisation

For an individual to include your organisation in a Will, he or she needs to know about your organisation. The higher your public profile, the more likely people are to think of your NPO when making a Will.

Marketing your organisation is useful for far more than just seeking bequests, and many of the tools that are used to market your organisation and its work are the same no matter whether annual gifts, major gifts or bequests are being solicited.

When a bequest fundraising programme is being instituted, it is a useful time to look at the marketing programme because a good public profile is useful in sourcing bequests. You can do this by:

- Developing a profile in the media as the source of informed comment on relevant issues.

- Producing easily accessible information about your organisation.

- Reporting your successes to the broader community.

- Maintaining an updated interactive website.

- Encouraging your staff and volunteers to promote your organisation through word-of-mouth contact.

- Gaining the endorsement of high-profile influential supporters.

- Providing opportunities for volunteer involvement.

Some organisations will not be interested in or able to build a high public profile. This doesn't mean that it will be impossible to seek and obtain bequests. Each organisation must decide what is best for it rather than try to conform to an external standard.

PUBLICISING BEQUEST GIVING

People need to know not just about your organisation and its work but also how they can leave money to you. In particular, current supporters should be made aware of the bequest giving opportunity because they are more likely to continue their support by leaving a bequest. Cold prospects, that is, those who have had no or little contact with your organisation, are less likely to support you by bequests. Users of the organisation's services should also be alerted to the opportunity because it may be an ideal way for them to "give back" to the organisation.

Others who should know about bequest possibilities include lawyers and solicitors, accountants, financial planners, and others who work with people planning their estates and preparing their Wills. All staff members as well as volunteers should be briefed about the opportunity to support the organisation. The more that people connected to the organisation know about the bequest opportunity, the more chance that they will take advantage of it.

Methods of disseminating information about bequest opportunities include:

- Website/Internet
- Newsletters
- Annual review/report
- Membership meetings
- Annual conference
- Fundraising or campaigning events
- Donor receptions or donor consultation seminars
- Direct mail
- Telemarketing
- Estate planning seminars
- Sectorwide bodies that promote such giving

Reviewer's Comment
Heavily publicise the usage of funds to encourage others. Don't be shy. Talk about what you have been able to achieve so far with bequests – success breeds success. Pictures, testimonials and stories are all means to communicate the positive effect the potential bequest donor could have on your organisation and/or fundraising project.

B equest fundraising, other than just sending out numbers of brochures, involves building a relationship with the prospective bequest donor.

The first step in building the relationship is knowing about your potential donors and initially finding out their potential giving capacity, or "qualifying" them. It often takes just as much time to identify, confirm and manage a bequest for 1,000 as it does for 1,000,000.

Some starting points for research:

- Use a web search engine to start your search about a particular person.

- Read the annual reports of a company that a potential donor works for or is a director of. (The reports cite directors' salaries and other useful information such as biographies of directors.)

- Check almanacs of jobs and salaries as a guide for the potential capacity of a donor.

- Check with government agencies to determine salaries of government employees. (In most countries, law requires this information to be publicly available.)

- Check local records to determine real estate property values.

- Ask other supporters of your organisation, who know the potential donor, for information.

- Hire companies that do prospect research.

Reviewer's Comment
Analyse your database to choose people who have a history of giving. If they have given before, they are likely to give again. Ensure you carefully research if a potential bequest donor has children and/or grandchildren because this is often the "sticking point" for why people choose not to leave a bequest to an NPO.

In some countries, privacy is governed by statute and is particularly important to consider when doing research. Every country is different, and you must familiarise yourself with the current legislative provisions for the collection and storage of personal information.

LEGAL AND TAX ISSUES

The Will is the primary document that ensures one's assets are distributed as intended on death. It dictates how the estate will be divided among the nominated family, individuals, and any organisations the deceased has chosen to support. A Will also allows individuals to name the executor whom they would like to carry out their wishes. Wills are changeable until the death of the donor, and, in some countries, amendments to the Will can be made after death.
In some countries, there will be arrangements called trusts, which take effect at death and operate much like a Will in distributing property and appointing representatives of the deceased donor. Bequests may be made as part of a trust. There may be other legal arrangements that people can enter into which are similar to a Will in disposing of an individual's property. The bequest fundraiser should take advice in his or her country from a knowledgeable lawyer or solicitor about what arrangements exist.

A bequest is a clause in a Will that directs money or property to a person or entity. There are four main types of bequests (although the names may be different in different countries, the principles are generally the same):

Specific bequests are defined gifts of assets such as a particular amount of money, a parcel of real estate, books, shares or jewellery. Specific bequests may also be called **general bequests**; if they are a percentage of an estate or percentage of an asset, they may be called **proportional bequests**.

Residuary bequests are gifts of the rest of an estate after specific bequests, debts, taxes and other expenses have been paid. A residuary bequest may be all of the remainder of any estate or a percentage of the remainder.

Contingent bequests are bequests that take effect after something else happens or doesn't happen. For example, a bequest that takes effect only if the spouse of the donor does not survive the donor is a contingent bequest. A contingent bequest can be either a specific bequest or a residuary bequest.

Continues on next page

Conditional bequests are bequests that take effect only if something else happens (for example, if an organisation agrees to build a building and name it after the donor). A conditional bequest can be either a specific bequest or a residuary bequest.

In some countries and some organisations, there will be other names for bequests, or bequests will be subdivided with different names. The crucial thing for the bequest fundraiser is not to assume that the above divisions are exactly what will be found in his or her country and to ascertain what bequests are called where he or she is working, how each bequest operates and how to explain it to potential donors.

In some countries, taxes need to be paid when someone dies. This tax may be called an estate tax or inheritance tax or some other name. There may also be a saving of tax when a bequest is made to a nonprofit organisation. In some places, the tax savings can be considerable and may be a strong motivation for making a donation to the NPO.

It is imperative that the fundraiser knows and understands the local tax laws as they relate to gifts at death to the organisation. Donors will ask tax-related questions, and you need to be prepared to explain to them the tax advantages of gifts to you. However, do not guess. If you are asked a question that you don't know, say as much and seek professional advice. Donors feel more confident with such a response rather than a confused and ultimately incorrect response.

Reviewer's Comment
It is also important that the fundraiser/NPO representative not be involved in the process of writing a Will in which the organisation is a beneficiary because such involvement will be perceived as unduly influencing the donor.

Information about how to make a bequest to the organisation in a Will is a vital piece of information. Every NPO seeking bequests should develop, with a knowledgeable lawyer or solicitor, clauses that can be provided to potential donors.

This is necessary because most donors will ask what clause they should use in their Will. It is crucial that the appropriate clauses are approved by a lawyer or solicitor who knows about this type of work and updated periodically as the law changes. Be prepared to provide information about a potential donor to the lawyer or solicitor or ask the professionals to speak directly to each other.

Materials to be given to potential bequest donors can be as simple as a brochure that outlines ways a benefactor can leave a bequest to your organisation or as detailed as an extensive package of information. Informational material should be available both in printed form and on the web.

The following information should be included:

- A brief overview of the organisation.

- Information about past bequests and the difference they have made, perhaps with a statement from a current supporter who is supporting the organisation in this way.

- Details about the organisation's strategic priorities (for at least 10-15 years) because it is possible that the gift may not take effect until some time in the future.

- Relevant tax information about benefits that may be available as a result of making a bequest.

- Information about making a Will and its importance in general.

- Sample bequest clauses for each type of bequest.

- Suggested percentages of estates or other amounts that the donor might want to consider leaving.

Continues on next page

MARKETING MATERIALS

- Mechanisms by which the donor may be thanked for support both during his or her lifetime and after death when the bequest takes effect.

- A statement of thanks.

- Frequently asked questions (FAQs).

- Contact information.

- Intention Form, in which the prospective donor can state his or her intention (either as a tear-off or a separate document).

The following starter sentences may be useful to begin your materials and, in fact, to frame their tone and focus:

- Please think about giving something….

- We cannot continue our work without your help….

- We rely entirely on the generosity of friends like you….

- Without your help, the gains of the past several years may evaporate….

- This is your chance to help (name of organisation) meet the challenges of coming years….

- Only a few people can make a difference and you are one of them….

- Your help will make a critical difference….

- In return for your help, you'll gain the satisfaction of….

Ensure the size of the typeface is suitable for the intended audience (should it be larger than usual if you are sending the brochure to older donors?) and the design is positive and uplifting. Plan to send your brochure to all relevant donors every year. Who is a relevant donor? Some categories to consider are all donors over a particular age, all donors who give a particular amount, or all donors who have expressed an interest in a particular activity of the organisation.

OTHER FORMS OF GIVING AT DEATH

As noted previously, different countries may have different legal arrangements that have the same result – the organisation receives a donation from an individual at the death of the individual or after the occurrence of some event that the donor prescribes. The following are a few examples of the types of arrangements that might exist. These may not be possible in all countries, and in some countries other types of arrangements will exist. This is not an exhaustive list, and the arrangements are not described in detail. Again, find out what is available in your country. Look at other organisations' literature; talk to people doing a similar job in other organisations; ask lawyers, accountants, financial planners.

Life Insurance Policies
Donors may donate new or existing life insurance policies whereby the donor's life is insured and the organisation is the recipient of the proceeds of the policy when the donor dies. Usually this arrangement not only provides tax benefits to the donor during his or her lifetime but also provides funds to the nonprofit when the donor dies.

Annuity Contracts
In the case of an annuity contract, the donor makes an arrangement with a financial institution whereby a sum of money is placed into an "account" (the contract), the donor receives predetermined payments during his or her lifetime, and the balance of the account remaining at the date of the donor's death goes to the organisation.

Residual Interest or Charitable Remainder Trust
In this arrangement, the donor establishes a trust but retains the right to the income of the trust or the use of the assets placed in the trust during his or her lifetime. At death, the remainder of the property is transferred to the nonprofit organisation and the donor's estate receives a tax benefit for the value of the amount that goes to the organisation.

Providing brochures and other information to potential bequest donors is only the start of the process.

Some people who receive the materials will want further information or to discuss, in person, the opportunity to support the organisation.

Other people will have been targeted by the organisation for face-to-face meetings to discuss making a bequest to the organisation.

A meeting in person to discuss leaving a bequest is desirable as the best way to effectively obtain a bequest or any large donation.

The main steps when planning and executing face-to-face solicitations, or Making the Ask, are:

- Ensure your research about the potential bequest donor is as complete as possible.

- Ask the potential donor to meet at a place convenient to him or her, usually at home.

- If possible, there should be at least two people from the organisation at the meeting – a staff member from the organisation and a volunteer who has already made a bequest to the organisation and knows the person being solicited.

  The staff member should be the person highest in the organisation commensurate with the hoped-for value of the bequest. The CEO or head of the organisation is most appropriate for the largest donations, the director of development or fundraising for significant donations.

- Those representing the organisation should be completely briefed on the individual being solicited, the organisation and any specific programmes for which funds are being sought, and relevant thank-you opportunities that will be available to the donor.

  They should know the legal and tax issues surrounding bequests and be able to answer any questions the potential donor might have.

Making the Ask

- Those who will attend the meeting should decide between or among themselves how the solicitation will be conducted, who will say what, and who will actually ask for the bequest to the organisation.

- Actually asking for the bequest can often be the hardest part of the meeting, and it is crucial that the person given this job actually does it. If you don't ask, you don't get.

- It should be agreed beforehand who will follow up the solicitation and what that follow-up will entail.

Reviewer's Comment
When visiting a potential bequest donor, always try to take something with you – a cake, organisational magazines, etc., because this helps break the ice.

Most significant bequests are sourced via direct personal contact.

Because the bequest is a future gift, the loyalty and commitment of benefactors must be maintained to ensure your organisation remains in the Will. This is referred to as stewarding the bequest or "pledge cuddling."

Means of stewardship could include:

- Ensuring those who have made bequests are invited to all donor thank-you events during their lifetimes.

- Keeping in regular contact with the donor via a schedule of visits to the donor or visits by the donor to the organisation, and also by letter, telephone or email.

- Keeping your bequest donor up-to-date with the work of the organisation and providing opportunities for him or her to stay involved.

- Publicising the donor's generosity (after checking that the donor wants his or her generosity publicly recognised).

Bequest Circles

Some organisations develop special programmes (often called bequest circles) for those who are leaving a bequest. These programmes can make the donors feel special and particularly valued. They can provide an opportunity for elderly bequest donors to get out, meet up with others, and both enjoy the conversation and learn useful information about the organisation. Other events can focus on thanking the donors, for their commitment to the organisation and for keeping the organisation in their minds. Thus, membership in bequest circles can build friendship and strengthen the relationship between the donors and the organisation. They can also encourage the members of the circle to identify other potential donors to the organisation through referrals.

A bequest donor may change his or her Will several times after making the initial decision to support an NPO. You need to ensure your cause remains a priority for donors, even when other circumstances in their lives change.

MANAGING INFORMATION

Maintaining up-to-date records of all relevant information about your bequest prospect or confirmed bequest donor can be easily accomplished using today's technology.

At a minimum, the database should enable you to:

- Load and update contact information.

- Describe past activity.

- Record current activity.

- Outline and prompt future actions.

- Run and access reports easily.

Keeping appropriate and accurate information at all stages of the relationship is a fundamental part of good customer care.

Some bequest decisions are made spontaneously by the donor and are prompted by personal experience or concern. Others come in response to an NPO's promotional activity. But many are motivated by an advisor or "influencer," that is, a third party from whom the donor takes advice. These advisors have direct access to your target audience. Promoting your cause to them can be an indirect means of reaching your primary audience.

The most common advisors are:

- Legal firms
- Financial planners
- Accountants
- Friends
- Relatives

Legal Firms
It is worth finding out which legal firms specialise in Wills and estate planning and ensuring they know about your organisation. In fact, it is worthwhile providing information to all legal firms.

Financial Planners and Accountants
These are professionals who may be able to act as conduits of information to potential bequest donors. Keep them supplied with up-to-date information and provide opportunities for them to familiarise themselves with your organisation.

You can keep all professionals in touch by:

- Producing annual bequest brochures they can provide to donors.

- Recognising and rewarding, with invitations to functions, those firms that have helped donors make bequests to your organisation.

- Directing prospective donors to firms that have helped your organisation in the past.

- Establishing a "recommended list" of legal advisors and accountants.

ADVISORS AND INFLUENCERS

- Writing thank-you letters to those who have been instrumental in sending a bequest donor to your organisation.

- Making personal visits.

- Sending small, inexpensive seasonal gifts.

- Publicising their assistance in newsletters, magazines, websites.

- Speaking at business/professional association functions they attend.

Friends and Relatives
As with any form of fundraising, people are more likely to give if asked by a friend or relative. Therefore, it is a good idea to look for potential bequest donors and influencers among your existing constituency or supporter base. People are more likely to make a bequest to an organisation they already have a relationship with and support morally or financially.

Publicise the availability of information about bequests to your supporters and promptly follow up any requests for information.

Various other professionals and community associations can be useful in helping you identify prospective donors. Consider, for example:

- Funeral homes

- Retirement homes

- Trusts

- Associations for senior citizens

While bequest work is about building relationships, the ultimate purpose is to be listed as a beneficiary in a Will, stay listed and receive a donation as a result of the bequest. It is an important feature of your fundraising programme to be able to measure your success at this.

Since receipt of the bequest traditionally takes 5-15 years from the time the Will is made, your actual income in a financial year is not the most reliable indicator of how your current bequest programme is performing. Success in the short term should be calculated on:

- The identification and relationship-building successes with key prospects.

- The identification and relationship-building successes with key influencers.

- The confirmed number of bequests.

Targets should be set in all these areas and results measured against them. Your technology should allow you to run simple reports or counts on these criteria.

CHARACTERISTICS OF BEQUEST FUNDRAISERS

Maturity and an ability to match the prospective donor's wishes with the needs of the organisation are the most important attributes for bequest fundraisers. Essential skills for the fundraiser charged with bequest fundraising are:

- A comprehensive understanding of the work of the NPO.

- Knowledge of the long-term strategic priorities of the NPO.

- Empathy with older people.

- Listening skills.

- An understanding of donor motivations.

- Donor relationship-building skills.

- Sound understanding of tax laws and Wills.

- Highest standard of ethics and ability to maintain confidentiality.

- Research skills.

- An ability to communicate well.

Some of these skills will be intrinsic to the person working in this field while others can be learned.

Tips for Successful Bequest Fundraising

- Don't confuse the relationship. Bequest donors are not your "friends"; they are donors to the organisation. Many donors may be elderly and may, therefore, be very vulnerable and lonely.

- Resources are limited so focus on those donors who can deliver the most benefit (in terms of funds and referrals) to your organisation.

- Never accept valuable gifts from bequest donors for your personal benefit.

- Adhere to the highest standards of conduct and confidentiality.

- Don't encourage or support bequest donors cutting family members from the Will. This can lead to the Will being challenged, and then a judgment call has to be made by your organisation as to the public relations wisdom of fighting the claim.

- Do discuss providing for loved ones first, before the nonprofit organisation.

- Don't give financial or legal advice. Always refer donors to appropriate professionals.

- Do ensure that at least two people in your organisation have a relationship with the bequest donor so the relationship is maintained despite staff turnover.

- Do develop a regular and varied schedule of contact mechanisms in order to move the relationship forward and maximize outcome with limited resources.

To be successful in bequest fundraising, you need to demonstrate a fundamental integrity. You must also have:

- A willingness to listen.

- A commitment to the organisation and its mission.

- An ability to build meaningful relationships.

- The ability to "close a deal."

- Above all, patience!